MORE SCIENCE PROJECTS

Heat

Written by Peter Lafferty

MARSHALL CAVENDISH WITHDRAWN
New York · London · Toronto · Sydney

Library Edition Published 1989

Published by Marshall Cavendish Corporation
147 West Merrick Road
Freeport, Long Island
N.Y. 11520

Printed in Italy by L.E.G.O. S.p.A., Vicenza

Library of Congress Cataloging-in-Publication Data

Lafferty, Peter.
  Marshall Cavendish More Science Projects Heat / written by Peter Lafferty : illustrated by Jeremy Grower, Sarah Leuton, Michael Strand.
    p. cm. – (Marshall Cavendish More Science Projects II : 3)
  Summary: Combines information and experiments to explore the world of heat.
  ISBN 1-85435-178-8. ISBN 1-85435-175-3 (set)
  1. Heat–Juvenile literature. 2. Heat–Experiments–Juvenile literature. [1. Heat, 2. Heat–Experiments. 3. Experiments.] I. Grower, Jeremy, ill. II. Leuton, Sarah, ill. III. Strand, Michael, IV Title. V. Series.
QC256.L34 1989
536' .078–dc20

89-7161
CIP
AC

PICTURE CREDITS
Key: t – Top, b – Bottom

Front Cover: Soames Summerhays / Science Photo Library

Page 6-7: ZEFA Picture Library
Page 10-11: The Photo Source
Page 13 t: Frank Lane Picture Agency
Page 13 b: The Mansell Collection
Page 17 t: Dr R Clarke and M Goff / Science Photo Library
Page 17 b: A De Menil / Science Photo Library
Page 21: NASA / Science Photo Library
Page 22-23: Simon Fraser / Science Photo Library
Page 24: Lloyds (Burton) Ltd / Steve Harley

Page 26: ZEFA Picture Agency
Page 27: David Parker / IMI / Univ. of Birmingham High TC Consortium / Science Photo Library
Page 28: Porterfield / Chickering / Science Photo Library
Page 32: Heini Schneebeli / Science Photo Library
Page 37: The Mansell Collection
Page 40: Martin Bond / Science Photo Library
Page 41: The Mansel Collection
Artwork by: Jeremy Gower / B L Kearley Ltd
          Sarah Leuton / B L Kearley Ltd
          Sallie Reason
          Michael Strand / B L Kearley

CONTENTS

GOLDEN RULES

This book contains lots of scientific facts, experiments and projects to help you find out more about heat and its strange properties. Whenever you try one of the experiments, make sure you read all about it before you start. You'll find a list of all the things you need, a step-by-step account of what to do, and finally an explanation of why and how your experiment works.

▶ Always watch what happens very carefully when you're doing an experiment and, if you find it doesn't work first time, *don't* give up.

Consider what could have gone wrong, and then read through the experiment once more. Check that everything is just right, and then try, try again. Real scientists may have to do an experiment several times before getting a worthwhile result.

▶ Because you will be such an active scientist, it's a good idea to start collecting for your laboratory. Nearly everything you need for the experiments can be found around your home. For example, bottles, cans, and pieces of cardboard and paper will often be used, so when you see your parents throwing away

■ GOOD SCIENTISTS... ■

ALWAYS THINK SAFETY FIRST

Famous scientists take precautions to avoid danger, so that they live to see their results and enjoy their fame. In any project or experiment, especially one you have thought up yourself, consider what it is you are trying to show and have a good idea of what should happen. Don't do any experiment without planning it "just to see what happens."

ALWAYS KEEP A NOTEBOOK

Whenever you are involved in scientific activity, keep your *Science Notebook* by your side and fill it with notes and sketches as you go along. Get into the habit of writing down your experiments and observations – your notes will come in handy in the future.

ALWAYS FOLLOW GOOD ADVICE

Advice and instructions, like the leaflets that come with pieces of equipment, should be read and understood. They are there for your safety and help. Good scientists think for themselves, but they are also wise and listen to what others have to say.

useful containers, offer to wash them and then add them to your supplies. General things like rulers, spoons for measuring, thumbtacks, and scissors will also come in handy. You'll also need colored pens and paper for lots of the experiments, as well as tape and glue. Finally, you will need a worktop for your experiments. It is a good idea to have it near a sink. Store your supplies in a nearby cupboard or cardboard box.

▶ Always let your parents know what you are doing. Sometimes you'll need their help. And when you need special equipment or chemicals, they'll know where to get them. Your parents may also help you to build wooden stands or nail things down when needed. And if you need to use matches, cut things out, or drill holes, **always** ask their permission first.

▶ Good scientists are clean and neat! They always remember to clear up when they have finished their experiments. So after you have completed your project, throw away anything you won't need again and clean everything else, ready for next time.

NEVER FOOL WITH HEAT

Never play with fires, stoves or kettles. They can cause severe burns. Always ask an adult to help you if you need to use heat of any kind. If you are using anything that runs on electricity, ask an adult to help. Remember, electricity can kill you.

NEVER PLAY WITH CHEMICALS

Avoid mixing chemicals and powders unless you are sure that you know what is going to happen, and always use small quantities. Dangerous chemical mixtures can explode or start a fire or burn your eyes and skin. Make sure any chemicals you keep are properly stored in jars and correctly labeled.

NEVER FOOL WITH HIGH-PRESSURE EQUIPMENT

Do not play with gas or liquids under pressure, especially in containers like aerosol cans – even if they seem empty. They can blow up in your face. Dispose of empty aerosols carefully and *never* put them in or near a fire.

WHAT IS HEAT?

Like most plants and animals, we need *heat* to live. The most important source of heat for the earth is the sun. But what is heat? What are its effects? How can it be measured?

In the eighteenth century, heat was thought to be a weightless fluid. Now it is known to be a form of energy – thermal energy – and is measured in units called *joules*, or B.T.U.s. The energy that generates heat comes from the movement of the tiny *molecules* and *atoms* that make up all matter. These particles are constantly on the move; they *vibrate* back and forth. When we touch a hot object, we feel the vibrations of the molecules and atoms as heat. Heat is the movement energy, or *kinetic energy*, of the molecules and atoms.

Heat can also be produced by hammering or rubbing. For example, if you hammer a nail, the kinetic energy of the hammer is changed into sound energy – a bang! – and thermal energy – the nail gets warm. If you haven't any gloves and it's a cold day, what do you do? You rub your hands together to warm them up! Here, the rubbing, or friction, is producing heat. In a similar way, if you rub two sticks together, the friction between them will release heat. If you continue rubbing, the sticks will generate so much heat that they will catch light. The intensity of heat produced is described as the *temperature* of the object.

Scientists have found that energy cannot be lost or gained: different types of energy can only be changed into one another. So, heat can be turned into electrical, chemical, mechanical or light energy, and vice versa. For example, what makes a car engine

The sun is the source of most of the heat on earth. The trees that are cut down for firewood needed sunlight to grow. Coal and oil, which we burn for heat, are formed from trees and plants that died millions of years ago and were buried beneath the ground.

run? The chemical energy of the gas is converted into heat; this *expands* the air, which pushes down the pistons in the engine. This produces the mechanical energy needed to drive the wheels of the car. So, chemical energy is converted to heat energy, which is then changed to mechanical energy.

PROJECT 1

Hot shot

When objects vibrate back and forth and bump into one another, the friction between them generates heat. You can show this quite easily. You will need a cardboard tube, two corks large enough to fit into the ends of the tube, a thermometer and some lead shot. A refrigerator or cold water to cool the shot would make the experiment more effective.

STEP 1

The corks must make an airtight seal in the tube. Cool the lead shot in the refrigerator or in cold water. Dry the shot thoroughly and gently pour it into the tube. Place the thermometer in the middle of the shot and note the temperature. Remove the thermometer and replace the cork.

STEP 2

Invert the tube at least one hundred times, shaking the shot very hard. Remove the cork from one end of the tube and gently push the thermometer into the shot. Measure the temperature again. If you shake the shot for an even longer time, does it get hotter?

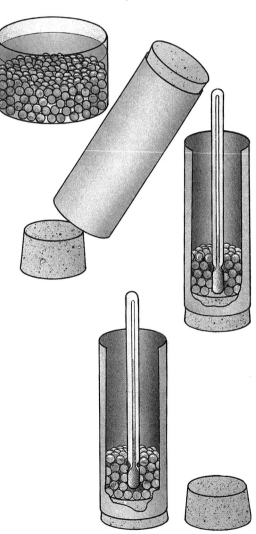

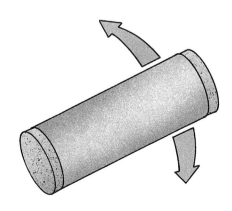

PROJECT 2

Hot pump

When air is compressed, or forced into a smaller space, the molecules move faster, hit one another and the air gets hot. And when air expands, or takes up more space, it gets cooler. You can use a bicycle pump to see this.

STEP 2

You will feel the pump get hot. This is because the air molecules are colliding with one another as they are made to move faster when the piston inside strikes them. This heats up the bottom of the pump.

STEP 1

Get a friend to work the pump while you hold one finger over the end of the tube where the air comes out. Wrap the fingers of your other hand around the bottom of the pump.

STEP 3

Release your finger slightly from the end of the tube. You will feel that the air coming from the tube is cool. As the air comes out of the pump, it expands. This means that the molecules are further apart and there are fewer collisions. So the air molecules move more slowly, and the air cools down.

9

HEAT ON THE MOVE

Heat can travel in three ways: *convection*, *conduction* and *radiation*. Convection and conduction can only take place where there is matter, made up of atoms and molecules, but radiant heat can travel through space.

The enormous energy generated inside the sun, the source of most of the earth's energy, streams out into space in every direction. As the space between the earth and the sun is almost a vacuum, the heat from the sun cannot travel by conduction or convection. Instead, it travels as waves of heat called radiant heat, or *infrared* radiation. All hot objects give out some radiant heat.

On earth, heat can travel in other ways. When gases or liquids are heated, they expand and become lighter, or less dense, and they rise above the colder gas or liquid. This movement of, for example, hot air rising and cold air sinking sets up convection currents. Such currents are seen on a large scale in the atmosphere and influence both the weather and wind patterns. Convection currents in the seas and oceans carry heat from the tropics to colder parts of the world. We use convection currents, on a smaller scale, in our homes. Household hot-water systems use them to circulate hot water in the storage tank. In central heating systems, the heat from radiators and duct outlets spreads around the room by convection currents in the air. These natural currents are often helped by a blower to maintain a good circulation.

The transfer of heat through a solid is by conduction. Some materials, such as metals, transfer heat very quickly. For example, if you place one end of a

poker in a fire, the other end soon becomes very hot. The heat from the fire has been transferred, or conducted, along the metal bar. Other materials are not such good heat conductors, so we use them to protect ourselves from heat or cold. Poor conductors of heat are called *insulators*.

11

CONVECTION

Have you seen a hot air balloon rising into the air? The balloon rises because the hot air inside it is lighter than the cool air outside. Hot air rises, even when it is not in a balloon. When a heater is turned on, warm air rises from it and spreads around the room. The air moves in a circle, rising as it heats up, and then falling as it cools.

Convection currents

These movements of air are called convection currents. Convection currents carry heat from one place to another. The trade winds are cool winds that blow from the north and south toward the equator. They are giant convection currents, caused by the air near the equator heating up and rising. Cool air flows toward the equator to take the place of the warm air.

Sea and land breezes are also convection currents. In the day, the land heats up faster than the sea, and so the air above the land heats up and rises. Cool air from the sea blows inland to take its place, forming a sea breeze. At night, the land cools faster than the sea, so a cool breeze blows out to sea.

In the early days of coal mining, convection currents helped to take fresh air to the miners working in the mines. Two shafts were sunk and a fire was started beneath one of them. The air above the fire was heated and rose up the shaft above the fire. Fresh air was drawn into the other shaft and ventilated the mine.

Here is a puzzle: Why can't a glassful of water be cooled by placing it on a block of ice? The answer is given on page 13.

uplift

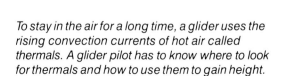

To stay in the air for a long time, a glider uses the rising convection currents of hot air called thermals. A glider pilot has to know where to look for thermals and how to use them to gain height.

Animals also use convection currents to carry excess heat away from their bodies. The fennec fox, which lives in Africa, has very large ears. Their surfaces act like radiators and give off heat to the outside air.

Liquids and gases

Convection takes place in both liquids and gases. Sometimes convection currents can be seen in a cup of hot milky coffee, or in a pan of water heating on the stove. Convection takes place because gases and liquids expand when they are heated. This expansion makes them less dense, so they rise.

When a liquid is heated, convection currents are set up. The warmer, less dense water rises to the top, and the cooler, heavier water sinks to the bottom to replace the warm water. This cool water is, in turn, heated and rises to continue the cycle.

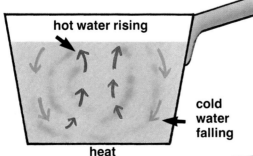

hot water rising

cold water falling

heat

SCIENCE DISCOVERY

Up and away!

The first balloon to fly used hot air to get lift. It made its first flight on June 15, 1783. Two French brothers, Joseph and Etienne Montgolfier, made the balloon from linen and paper. It was about 10 yards (10 m) across. An opening at the bottom was held over a fire of straw and rags. The balloon soon filled with smoke and hot air and rose to a height of about 6,000 feet (1,800 m).

In September, 1783, they showed their balloon to the King and Queen of France. The balloon carried three passengers, a sheep, a cockerel and a duck. After a short flight, the animals landed safely. On November 21, 1783, the first human passengers were carried in a balloon. The flight lasted 25 minutes and covered a distance of 5½ miles (9 km).

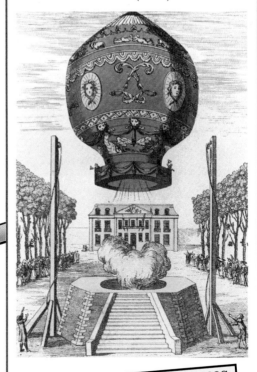

Answer: Any warm water in the glass rises to the top and is not cooled because it always stays at the top away from the ice.

13

CONDUCTION

If you put a pan of water on a stove, the water will heat up quickly. This is because the heat flows from the hot burner through the metal pan and into the water. This process is called the conduction of heat. Conduction is the way heat travels through solids.

But why?

Heat flows through a solid because the molecules jostle, or bump into each other, as they heat up. When the bottom of a pan is heated on the stove, the molecules at the bottom of the pan start to vibrate. They start to move backward and forward very rapidly. The hotter the bottom of the pan gets, the more rapidly the molecules vibrate. These vibrating molecules bump into the molecules next to them, a little farther from the heat. These molecules start to vibrate as well. In turn, they bump against

SCIENCE PROJECT

Good conductor, poor conductor

Some materials are better conductors than others. You can test this for yourself. You will need a piece of copper wire, a piece of steel wire, a wooden rod and a plastic rod, all the same length and thickness, a candle, four long steel pins, matches, a small bowl, modeling clay, very hot water and a watch.

Light the candle and place a drop of wax on the end of each of the rods. Place a pin in the wax so that the tip is just on the top of the rod, and hold it there until the wax solidifies. Place four pieces of clay at intervals around the top of the bowl.

Place the four rods in the bowl and attach them with the clay. Very carefully, pour the very hot water into the bowl. Ask an adult to help you. As the heat travels through the rods, they become hot, the wax melts and the pin falls off. Time how long it takes for the pins to fall off. Is the good conductor the rod with the longest or shortest time?

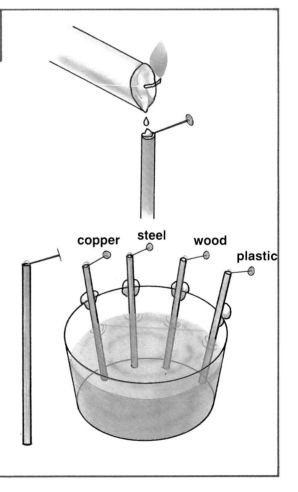

copper steel wood plastic

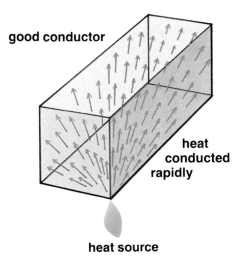

good conductor

heat conducted rapidly

heat source

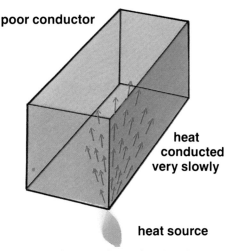

poor conductor

heat conducted very slowly

heat source

In good conductors, the molecules in the material are free to vibrate easily, and the heat can be passed rapidly from one molecule to the next. In

poor conductors, the molecules do not vibrate so easily, so heat is transferred more slowly.

their neighbors and start them moving. Soon, when all the pan has heated up, all the molecules in the pan are vibrating faster.

Some substances are better conductors than others. Metals, like copper, iron and steel, are good conductors. These materials also allow

electricity to flow easily through them. They are often made into electric wires. Other substances, such as rubber, are bad conductors. Heat does not flow easily through them. Materials that do not conduct heat easily are called insulators.

When the engines of cars run, heat is produced. This heat has to be dispersed; otherwise, the engine would overheat. Car radiators are filled with water, which is used to cool the engine and therefore gets hot. The metal radiator has a large surface area and so, as well as being a good heat conductor, the heat is easily carried

away by convection as air moves around the radiator. This means that the water in the radiator does not boil and overheat the engine.

RADIATION

You know that heat comes to us from the sun. If you stand outside on a sunny day you can feel the sun's heat. The heat is traveling across space as rays, or radiation. Heat rays are very like light rays. They both travel at the same speed, 200,000 miles (300,000 km) per second, and take just over eight minutes to travel to the earth, a distance of about 100,000,000 miles (150,000,000 km).

Infrared rays

William Herschel, a famous astronomer, discovered infrared rays in about 1800. Using a prism, he bent the rays of the sun into the colors of the spectrum. He noticed that heat was coming from just beyond red light at the end of the spectrum. He decided that, in the sunlight, there must be invisible rays that carried heat. He called them infrared rays.

SCIENCE FACTFILE

Summer is hotter than winter because the earth is tilted as it travels around the sun. Northern countries are tilted toward the sun in June and July, so that the sun is almost overhead. The sun's rays are spread over a small area, and they only have to pass through a thin layer of the atmosphere. So, the rays keep the temperature high. In winter, the earth is tilted away from the sun, so that the sun is not overhead and its warmth is spread out. Also, the rays have to pass through a thicker layer of the atmosphere, so the temperature is not raised as much as in summer.

Infrared rays are not only given out by very hot things, like the sun or an electric heater. They are given out by all hot objects, including our bodies. Radiant heat, like light, can be reflected, absorbed or transferred by matter. Infrared waves only give up their heat energy when they are absorbed by an object.

In space, there is no air to protect astronauts from the heat of the sun. So their space suits and the space shuttle are painted white to reflect the sun's rays. This is an old trick which is well-known to people who live in hot climates. They paint their houses

---

SCIENCE PROJECT

Good radiators or bad?

Some surfaces are better radiators than others. See for yourself using two identical tin cans. Remove the label from both cans. Paint one with black paint and fill both with hot water. Then bring the shiny can near your cheek. Can you feel the heat radiated by the can? Next bring the black can near your cheek. Can you notice any difference? You should find that the black tin radiates more heat. A shiny object is a bad radiator.

Infrared radiation is a form of electromagnetic radiation and is found just beyond the red light at the end of the spectrum.

SCIENCE IN ACTION

Seeing red

Doctors can use heat rays to detect some diseases. Using film that is sensitive to infrared radiation, they take a photograph of the patient. It shows the temperature of different parts of the patient's body. Cool parts of the body show up as blue, or purple. The hottest parts are shown as white or red. Some diseases, like arthritis and cancer, make the diseased parts hotter. This shows up on the infrared photograph.

white and often wear white clothes for the same reason.

Getting through glass

The inside of a greenhouse is hotter than the air outside because the infrared rays from the very hot sun have a short wavelength and can travel through glass. The plants and soil inside absorb these rays and become warm. As they warm up, they also give out infrared rays. However, as the plants and soil are not very hot, the rays have a longer wavelength and cannot pass through the glass. They are trapped inside the greenhouse and raise the temperature inside. This is called the greenhouse effect.

Helpful rays

Infrared rays can help you change television channels. You use a remote control device that gives off infrared rays. The television set is able to pick up these rays. It changes channels when it detects an infrared signal. Some burglar alarms give out a beam of infrared rays. If anything moves through the infrared beam, the alarm goes off. Doctors treat muscle pains with infrared rays. The heat carried by the rays travels into the muscle and eases the pain.

A firefighter wears a special suit when he puts out a fire. The suit is made of asbestos, which is a poor conductor of heat. Its silvery surface reflects heat so that it is not absorbed.

PROJECT 3

Black or white?

What color clothes would you wear in a hot climate? This experiment will help you find the best clothes. You will need two similar thermometers and some squares of cloth, all the same size, but in different colors. Black and white are good colors for this experiment.

STEP 1

Lay the thermometers on the ground near each other. It is best to try this experiment on a sunny day. Leave the thermometers for ten minutes. Then read the temperatures.

STEP 2

Cover one thermometer with a piece of black cloth and the other with a piece of white cloth. Leave them in the sunshine for about 20 minutes.

STEP 3

Remove the cloth and read the temperatures. Under which cloth is the temperature higher? Which cloth absorbs most of the sun's heat rays?

STEP 4

Now try the experiment with different colors. Do your discoveries help you to decide which clothes to wear in a hot climate? What colors would you wear in a cold climate?

PROJECT 4

Twisting snake

Here is a simple experiment to try. You will need some stiff paper, scissors, needle and thread, a colored pencil and a lamp or radiator.

STEP 1

Cut a circle from a piece of stiff paper. Draw a spiral on the paper, gradually making it thinner as it winds its way into the center. Make the spiral look like a snake by drawing a snake's head at the outer end of the spiral. Draw zigzag lines along the snake's back.

STEP 2

Cut around the spiral. Thread the needle. Tie a thick knot in one end of the thread and push the needle through the tail of the snake. Hang the snake by the thread in its tail, and it will spread out into a coil.

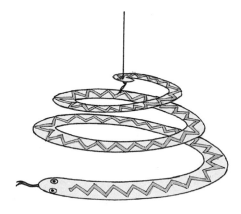

STEP 3

Hold the snake by the thread above a shining table lamp, or a hot radiator. Convection currents will rise from the warm lamp or radiator. These currents will make the snake turn round and round.

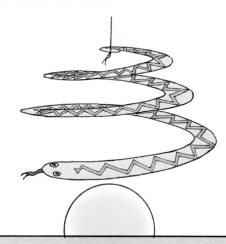

INSULATION

Poor conductors of heat, such as wood, rubber and plastic, are known as heat insulators. Insulators are used to stop heat from flowing. The handle of a pan is made from an insulator so that you can pick up the hot pan without getting burned. Most gases and liquids are good insulators and poor conductors of heat. Heat travels through liquids and gases by convection, not conduction.

Keeping warm

In cold weather, we wear wool clothing to stop heat from being lost from the body. Wool is a good insulator because the air trapped between the strands of wool is a poor conductor and, as the air cannot move, convection cannot take place. This insulation keeps out cold and prevents heat from being lost from the body. Sheep keep warm in the same way, and furry animals are kept warm by the layer of air trapped in their coats.

Deep-sea divers wear tight-fitting rubber clothes, a good insulator. The layer of air trapped between the skin and rubber also helps to keep the body heat in and insulates the diver against the cold.

We use similar methods of insulation to keep our homes warm. A layer of insulating material such as foam or fiberglass is put in the walls of houses, and in the roof, to prevent heat from flowing out. Not only is the material used a poor conductor of

SCIENCE PROJECT

How can you stop heat from being lost from an object? One way is to cover it with an insulator. You can easily prove this for yourself. Wash two empty metal cans and remove their labels. Leave one uncovered and place the other in a thick, wool sock. Half-fill each can carefully with very hot water. Using a thermometer, take the temperature of the water every two or three minutes. Which of the cans of water cools more quickly? You could plot your results on a graph. Why do you think the wool sock is a good insulator?

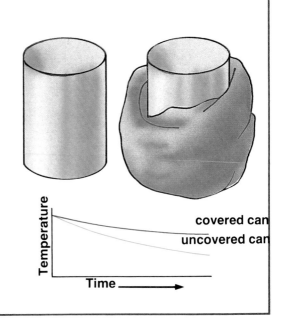

SCIENCE IN ACTION

Vital protection

When the space shuttle returns to earth, it has to enter the atmosphere, the layer of air that surrounds the earth. It hits the top layers of the atmosphere at great speed. This heats the bottom of the shuttle to a very high temperature. The shuttle and the astronauts inside have to be protected from the heat. A layer of special glazed tiles, is put on the bottom of the shuttle. They are very poor conductors of heat. They stop the heat from reaching the astronauts. Ceramics are used in some modern stoves.

heat, but the layer of air trapped in the fibers acts as another layer of insulation. Some window panes are built with two panes of glass, with air between the panes. This stops heat from escaping through the window, because the trapped air can neither conduct nor convect heat, and glass is a poor conductor.

Keeping cool

A refrigerator has insulation material around it to keep it cold. The insulation stops heat from being conducted to the inside from the warmer room. Furnace workers wear clothes made from asbestos, a good insulator, to protect them from the heat of the fire.

*A **vacuum bottle** is made to keep in as much heat or cold as possible. The glass bottle has two walls. The air has been removed from between the walls to create a vacuum. This stops heat from traveling by conduction. The bottle is silvered inside to reflect heat so that it does not pass in or out by radiation.*

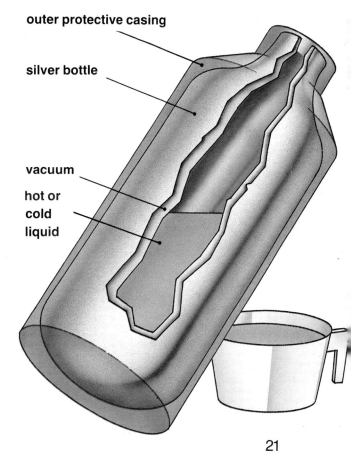

outer protective casing

silver bottle

vacuum

hot or cold liquid

TEMPERATURE

Is it a hot day today? You can answer this question easily. You don't have to be exact. If the day feels hot to you, you would answer, "Yes." But someone else might answer, "No, it is not hot today" if they like hot weather. These answers would not satisfy a scientist. Scientists like to have exact answers. This is why scientists like to measure the things they study.

How do you measure how hot it is? You measure temperature using an instrument called a *thermometer*. The temperature of an object is a measure of how hot or cold it is. For example, an ice cube is colder than boiling water. So the temperature of the cube is lower than the temperature of the water. It is hotter in the Sahara Desert than in the Antarctic, so the temperature is higher there.

Using special thermometers, a scientist can measure the temperatures of very hot or cold places. They have calculated that the surface of the sun is 200 times hotter than a summer day. Inside the sun, it is 2000 times hotter still. In the depths of outer space far from the sun, it is three times colder than in the Antarctic. This is close to the lowest temperature possible – *absolute zero*.

There is a difference, however, between the temperature of an object and the amount of heat it contains. The heat in an object depends on both its temperature and the amount of matter it contains. A small object which is very hot does not hold as much

heat as a large object that is not so hot. Imagine a needle that has been heated until it is red hot and a large pan of boiling water. The temperature of the

The amount of heat in an object depends on its size as well as its temperature. An iceberg in the Antarctic is very cold. Its temperature is low. Yet even an iceberg contains heat. A large iceberg contains enough heat to boil plenty of water, if only it could be harnessed.

needle is much higher than that of the water. But there is less heat in the needle than in the hot water. You could prove this by dropping the hot needle into a pan of cold water. The water would be heated up slightly, but it would not *boil*. There is not enough heat in the needle to boil a pan of water.

MEASURING TEMPERATURE

One way to find out if something is hot or cold is simply to touch it. But this method is not accurate enough for scientists because our skin is not sensitive to small temperature changes.

Using thermometers

Thermometers are used to measure temperatures accurately. They work because liquids expand, or increase in size, when they are heated. We measure the temperature by seeing how much the liquid expands.

A silver-colored liquid metal called mercury is used in some thermometers. It is used because it expands and *contracts* evenly. Some thermometers use alcohol (with a red dye added to it as it is colorless) because it has a lower freezing point and can be used in conditions where mercury would freeze.

All thermometers are calibrated using two fixed points. The lower fixed point marks the point to which the liquid contracts when the thermometer is placed in ice-cold water; the higher fixed point marks the point to which the liquid expands when the thermometer is placed in boiling water. An even scale is marked between the two points. When measuring the temperature of, for example, the air, the mercury or alcohol expands, moving up the tube until it reaches the same temperature as the air outside. This temperature can then be read on the scale.

This worker is measuring the temperature of an iron furnace using an instrument called a pyrometer. A pyrometer is used to measure high temperatures from a distance. It calculates the temperature of the furnace from its color.

SCIENCE PROJECT

Hot or cold?

It is easy to confuse our sense of heat. Try this experiment. Dip one hand into a bowl of ice-cold water, and the other into a bowl of fairly hot water. Leave your hands in

Celsius, Fahrenheit and Kelvin

In the *Fahrenheit* scale, the difference between these two points is divided into 180 parts, or degrees. The temperature of melting ice is marked as 32°F. The temperature of boiling water is 212°F. It is called the Fahrenheit scale, after a German scientist, Gabriel Fahrenheit, who invented it.

On the *Celsius*, or *centigrade*, scale, named after a Swedish scientist, Anders Celsius, the temperature of icy water is 0°C, and that of boiling water is 100°C.

Lord Kelvin invented the *Kelvin* scale of temperature based on the coldest possible temperature, absolute zero, −459°F [−273°C (0 K)]. One Kelvin is equal to 33.8°F (1°C). On the Kelvin scale, 32°F (0°C) becomes 273 K, and 212°F (100°C), 373 K.

the water for about a minute. Quickly dry your hands and put them both into a bowl of warm water. The hand that has been in the hot water will feel cold, and the hand that has been in the cold water will feel hot. This shows how unreliable it is to judge temperatures by touch.

Here are two different thermometers. The household thermometer on the right contains alcohol, with a red dye added to make it easy to see. The doctor's thermometer on the left contains mercury. When the thermometer is put into your mouth, the mercury expands and goes up the tube. It forces its way past the narrow section of the tube. When the thermometer is taken from your mouth, the mercury above the narrow section cannot flow back into the bulb. It is left in the tube to show what your temperature was. The thermometer must be shaken to get all the mercury back into the bulb before it can be used again.

HIGH AND LOW

The hottest place in the universe is inside a star. Deep inside some stars, the temperature reaches over 500,000,000°F (300,000,000°C). Even the sun, which is a rather small and average yellow star, is very hot. The temperature at its surface is 11,000°F (6,000°C), and at the center the temperature reaches 25,000,000°F (14,000,000°C). Scientists can tell the temperature of a star from its color. A blue star is very hot, a white star is cooler, and a red star is coolest of all.

The enormous heat inside a star rips apart the atoms of the materials, mainly hydrogen, that make up the stars. A star consists of a glowing ball of gas made of rapidly moving electrons and protons. These are the small particles that made up the hydrogen atoms before they were ripped apart by the great heat. The gas of electrons and protons found inside a star is called plasma.

Absolute zero

In deepest space, far away from any star, the temperature is very different. It is about –450°F (–270°C). This is cold enough to freeze instantly anything unlucky enough to find itself in space. It is close to the lowest temperature possible, which is called absolute zero.

Absolute zero is the temperature at which, in theory, there is no heat at all. All the atoms or molecules in a body

A nuclear bomb explodes with the power of millions of tons of ordinary explosive. Inside the ball of fire, the temperature is around 200,000,000°F (100,000,000°C). Some stars are three times hotter at their center!

Strange effects can be produced by very low temperatures. This small cylinder is floating in midair. It has been cooled by liquid nitrogen to –310°F (–190°C). At this temperature, a very strong electric current flows in the cylinder, creating a powerful magnetic field which supports it in midair. This is called "magnetic levitation."

stop moving. They are completely still. Absolute zero is a temperature of –459.4°F (–273.16°C). Nothing can be colder than this temperature. This temperature has never been reached, as all matter contains some heat.

Believe it or not!

At very low temperatures, strange things happen. Gases, like hydrogen or oxygen, freeze solid. Helium, a gas at normal temperatures, turns into a liquid called superfluid at –450°F (–270°C). It can flow uphill! If an empty cup is lowered into superfluid helium, the helium flows up the outside of the cup, and into the cup. If the cup is then lifted out of the helium, the liquid in the cup flows up the inside of the cup and over the top, back into the original container.

SCIENCE IN ACTION

Power for the future

Scientists are trying to make power in the same way the sun makes its heat and light. The process is called nuclear fusion. In this process, the tiny central parts, called nuclei, of hydrogen atoms join together to form helium. Enormous amounts of energy are released when this happens. If nuclear fusion could be made to work, the world would never run out of energy. Hydrogen from sea water could be used as fuel.

But there are still many problems to be solved. The hydrogen nuclei have to be heated to 200 million °F (100 million °C) before they will join together. Scientists are building huge machines, called fusion reactors, to produce these enormous temperatures. The hot gas or plasma produced is contained in a powerful magnetic field. The magnetism is produced by huge electric currents flowing through coils of wire embedded in a doughnut-shaped concrete wall.

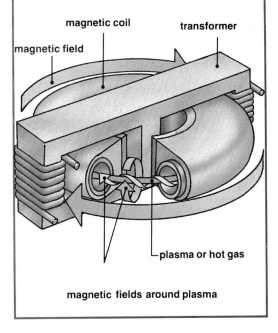

magnetic coil   transformer

magnetic field

plasma or hot gas

magnetic fields around plasma

BOILING AND FREEZING

If you heat water, the molecules vibrate more and more swiftly. Eventually, some molecules have so much energy that they fly through the surface of the water. We say the water has boiled. When the water reaches boiling point, it turns first to an invisible gas. The cloud of steam you see is the gas, or water vapor, *condensing* back into water on contact with the colder air above.

Industrial processes often use heat to purify chemicals. For example, in an oil refinery, the crude oil is heated in a fractionating column until it vaporizes. The fractions that vaporize first, such as fuel gas and gasoline, rise to the top of the column and are piped out. Kerosene, heating oil and lubricating oil vaporize at higher temperatures and don't rise as far, and are piped out lower down.

Vanishing molecules

Evaporation is like slow boiling. Put a drop of water on a plate, and leave it for a while in a warm place. Eventually, the drop will vanish. The molecules in the water have absorbed warmth and escaped into the air.

Try this test. Wet your hand and wave it around in the air. Your hand will feel cold. This is because the water is evaporating. It takes the heat it needs to evaporate from your hand, which then feels cold. The faster the water evaporates, the colder your hand feels.

The spray used by a football trainer kills pain by evaporation. The chemicals in the spray evaporate very quickly and rapidly cool down the muscles that have been sprayed. The muscles are so cold that they do not feel pain. Dentists use a similar spray to prevent pain in their patients' mouths.

Freezing liquids

Freezing is the opposite of *melting*. When a liquid cools down, its molecules move more and more slowly. Eventually, they are moving so slowly that they cluster together, and the liquid freezes, or *solidifies*. Sometimes crystals form when a liquid freezes. The crystals

A geyser shoots a column of boiling water and steam high into the air. Geysers are found in volcanic regions where water under pressure deep within the earth boils. In New Zealand and California, steam from geysers is used to make electricity.

The water molecules in ice can only move slightly. They are held together by strong bonds. If ice is heated, the bonds break. The ice melts to make water. As the water is heated, the molecules move more and more. Eventually, they move so much that they burst through the surface of the water, producing steam. In the steam, the molecules are even farther apart and move with great speed.

often have beautiful shapes. The shapes occur because the molecules build up regular patterns as they cluster together.

Frozen objects can be melted by pressure as well as heat, because increased pressure lowers the melting point. If pressure, like a heavy weight, is put on ice, the ice melts. Ice is slippery for skaters because the pressure of the blade and friction melts the ice.

SCIENCE IN ACTION

Cool it!

Refrigerators cool by using evaporation. In refrigerators, a liquid called a refrigerant flows through a pipe. This liquid evaporates very easily. The liquid is compressed to a high pressure in one section of the refrigerator. The compressed liquid then flows into a part of the refrigerator where the pressure is low. Here the liquid evaporates very rapidly, forming a gas. This fast evaporation takes the heat from the inside of the refrigerator as heat always flows from hot areas to colder areas. The gas is then compressed again to turn it back into a liquid, and used again. This method of cooling is used in all electric refrigerators.

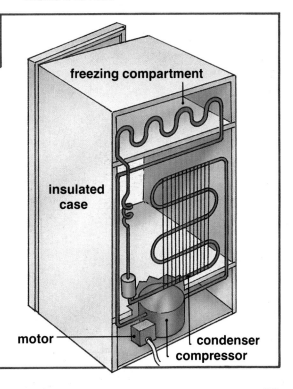

freezing compartment

insulated case

motor

condenser

compressor

PROJECT · PROJECT · PROJECT · PRO
ROJECT · PROJECT · PROJECT · PROJE
CT · PROJECT · PROJECT · PROJ
ECT · PROJECT · PROJE
PRO
JECT
· PRO
JECT

PROJECT 5

A drinking straw thermometer

You can make a simple thermometer easily. You need a thin plastic drinking straw, some modeling clay, a few drops of ink or poster paint, a waterproof marker, a cup, some hot water, and some icy water.

STEP 1

Put a few drops of ink or paint into half a cup of water to make a colored liquid. Dip one end of the straw into the liquid until it holds about ½ inch (1 cm) of liquid.

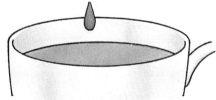

STEP 2

Push a small ball of clay onto the other end of the straw. Lift the straw out of the cup and stand it upright with the clay as its base at the bottom. The liquid in the straw will stay at the top of the straw.

STEP 3

Wiggle the straw gently until the liquid in the straw moves down the straw by about 2 inches (5 cm).

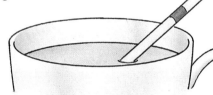

STEP 4

You can now "calibrate" your thermometer by putting scale marks on it. All instruments have to be calibrated before they can be used. Place the thermometer in a cup of hot water, with the clay end down. Mark the straw with a waterproof marker to show how high the ink rises in the straw.

STEP 5

Put the thermometer into a cup of icy water. As the air cools down and contracts, the liquid will move down the straw. Mark the straw to show where the ink moves. You now have two fixed points and can use your thermometer to compare the temperature of, say, your bathwater, a sunny window sill, inside a refrigerator, and anywhere else you think of.

The freezing and boiling point of water can be altered quite easily. Try these simple experiments for yourself.

PROJECT 6

Lowering the freezing point and raising the boiling point

You will need some small pieces of ice and some larger ice cubes, a small container, salt, a thermometer and the stove.

STEP 1

Put some of the small pieces of ice in the container and stir them until the ice melts. Take the temperature of the icy water. Repeat the experiment, but this time sprinkle salt on the ice before it melts. What do you find? Why do you think people put salt on icy roads in the winter?

ice and water   **salt, ice and water**

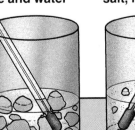

STEP 2

Take the two large ice cubes and press them together as hard as you can and then gently release the pressure. What has happened? Squeezing has increased the pressure, causing the ice to melt. When you release the pressure, the ice refreezes, "sticking" the ice cubes together. What do you think happens when you make snowballs?

STEP 3

Put some water in a pan and heat it on a stove until it boils. Measure the temperature of the water. Repeat the experiment, but add some salt before you boil the water. What do you find? Why do potatoes cook faster if you put salt in the water?

boiling water   boiling salt water

Remember: impurities or increased pressure lowers the melting point or raises the boiling point of water.

CHANGED BY HEAT

All things change when they are heated. Sometimes they just change their state, for example from a liquid to a solid, and sometimes a new substance is produced.

Heat causes most things to expand. Solids get larger when they are heated and smaller when they are cooled. Convection currents that carry heat in liquids and gases move because the liquid or gas expands, and becomes less dense, when heated.

Heat can produce dramatic changes of state. An ice cube melts when heated. It changes from a solid to a liquid. If water is boiled, it changes into a gas, water vapor. All substances, even metals like tin and iron, melt and boil if they are heated enough.

When water vapor cools, we see the opposite effect. The vapor condenses into water droplets in the air, which you see as steam, and collects as liquid water. Further cooling solidifies the water and changes it into ice. Almost all gases become a liquid and then a solid if they are cooled enough. Air, for example, becomes a solid if it is cooled to very low temperatures.

Melting, boiling and expanding are called *physical changes*. They can be reversed by cooling or vice versa. But some changes induced by heat, called *chemical changes*, cannot be reversed.

A chemical change occurs when a new substance is produced. If you burn a match, a new material, charcoal, is produced. You cannot turn the charcoal back into a match. Burning is

a chemical change. So is cooking. When you cook a piece of meat, the heat changes the chemicals in the meat. New ones are produced that

Very high temperatures are used in steel foundries to melt the crude pig iron. The carbon in the pig iron, which makes it brittle, is removed when it combines with oxygen in the air to form carbon dioxide. The pure steel is then tapped off.

make the meat tastier and easier to eat. Industrial chemists heat cheap and plentiful materials to change them into useful new ones. For example, the very high temperatures produced in blast furnaces are used to make steel from pig iron and glass from sand, soda and limestone.

GETTING BIGGER

Most solids, liquids and gases expand when they are heated and contract when they are cooled. This is because the atoms and molecules from which they are formed move more rapidly or more slowly when they are heated or cooled (see pages 6, 10 and 14). These are all physical changes. For the same increase in temperature, gases expand about a hundred times more than solids. Also, different kinds of substances expand by different amounts for the same rise in temperature. These important facts are taken into account by engineers when they design buildings or equipment.

All around you

You can see many examples of expansion in solids every day. On hot days, telephone wires on poles along the street sag because they have expanded. In winter, they contract, or get shorter. Bridges made of steel have gaps left in them to allow for expansion. If the bridge were firmly bolted down at each end, it might buckle on a hot day. Railroad tracks used to have small gaps between the rails for the same reason.

Expansion and contraction, and the enormous forces exerted by them, can cause great damage. On occasions, however, they can be very useful. If two metal strips, such as brass and iron, are welded together, they form a bimetallic strip. When heated, the brass expands more than the iron and in so doing becomes longer, making the strip bend. This fact is used in the control switches of thermostats, which are used to maintain an even temperature.

SCIENCE IN ACTION

Why your iron stays hot

Many thermostats depend on the fact that different materials expand by different amounts when they are heated. They are used to keep something at the same temperature, without getting too hot or too cold.

In an electric iron, for example, a bimetallic strip made from iron and brass forms part of the electric circuit which heats the element at the base of the iron. The brass expands and contracts more with changes in temperature than the iron, and so the strip bends. When the strip is straight, it touches an electrical contact,

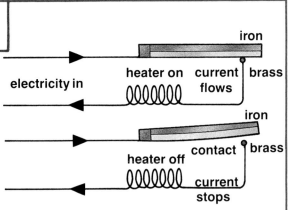

the circuit is complete and the current flows and heats the iron. When it bends away from the contact, the circuit is broken, the current does not flow and the iron cools down.

Expanding bubbles

You can easily prove that gases expand when they are heated. Make a rich lather by rubbing soap and water between your hands. Carefully put a bubble across the neck of a small empty plastic bottle. Hold the bottle in your warm hands, or place it in a bowl of hot water. What happens to the size of the bubble? What would happen if you put the bottle in a bowl of cold water?

Under water

Most liquids expand as they get hotter and contract as they get cooler, a fact that is used in all thermometers (see page 24). But water behaves strangely. When ice cold water is heated gently, it contracts until the temperature rises to 39.2°F (4°C). Then it starts to expand like normal substances. This means that water takes up the least space and is most dense at 39.2°F (4°C). This

Water is densest at 39.2°F (4°C). Because this dense water falls to the bottom of the pond, the bottom stays at 39.2°F (4°C) even when the top freezes.

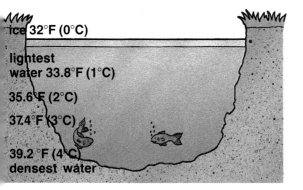

ice 32°F (0°C)

lightest
water 33.8°F (1°C)

35.6°F (2°C)

37.4°F (3°C)

39.2°F (4°C)
densest water

fact helps fish live in winter. When a pond freezes, the dense water, which is a little warmer, sinks to the bottom of the pond, and the ice, which is less dense, floats at the top. Fish can live comfortably in this water even when the surface of the pond is completely covered with ice. Icebergs float for the same reason: the ice is less dense than the cold water around it.

Expanding gases

Gases expand most of all. You can see how much gases expand by putting a blown-up balloon into the refrigerator. Measure the size of the balloon before you put it in. After about ten minutes, take the balloon out. Measure its size again. Then put the balloon into the sun. After ten minutes, measure its size again.

The fact that gases expand so much when they are heated has been widely used by mankind. All heat engines, from steam engines to rocket engines, operate by the expansion of gases (see page 36).

ENGINES AT WORK

Until about 300 years ago, there were no engines. The only machines for producing power were windmills and watermills. The *steam engine* was the first real engine. At first, steam engines were used to pump water out of mines. Later, they were used to pull locomotives on railroads. There were even steam-driven automobiles and motorcycles.

Steam engines

In a steam engine, water is heated until steam is produced. The hot steam flows into a round tube called a cylinder. Here, the steam pushes a piston backward and forward. The piston moves forward when steam flows into one end of the cylinder, and backward when the steam flows into the other end. The piston is connected by rods to the wheels of the locomotive. The back and forth movement of the piston makes the wheels go around.

Internal combustion engines

Steam engines were large and needed a lot of fuel, so inventors searched for better engines. One early design for an engine used gunpowder as a fuel. The gunpowder exploded inside the cylinder, and the hot gases produced by the explosion pushed the piston along. Other designs burned gas to push the piston. These engines are called *internal combustion engines*. They burn a fuel such as gasoline inside the 'engine to produce power.

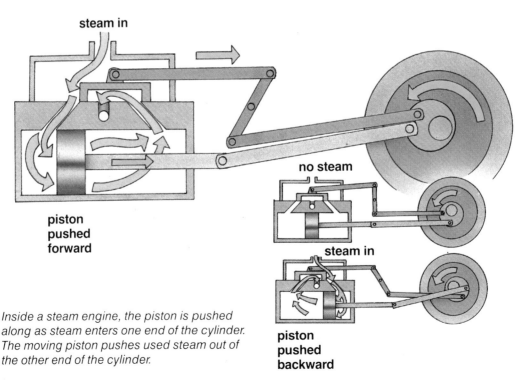

steam in

piston
pushed
forward

no steam

steam in

piston
pushed
backward

Inside a steam engine, the piston is pushed along as steam enters one end of the cylinder. The moving piston pushes used steam out of the other end of the cylinder.

SCIENCE IN ACTION

Gas and air mixture is drawn into the cylinder. Inlet valve is open. Exhaust valve is closed.

Both valves closed. Piston rises and gas/air mixture is compressed.

Valves closed. Spark from spark plug ignites gas/air mixture. Mixture explodes and the piston is forced down.

Exhaust valve opens. Burnt gases are pushed out.

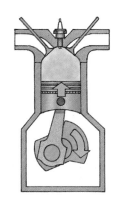 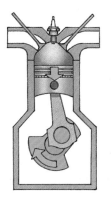 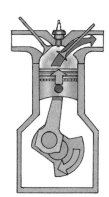

How the gasoline engine works

The automobile engine is an internal combustion engine that uses gasoline as a fuel. It is called a four-stroke engine because it produces its power in four steps, or strokes. At the first stroke, a mixture of fuel and air is fed into the engine. At the second stroke, the mixture is squashed into a smaller space, or compressed. At the third stroke, the mixture is exploded and, at the fourth stroke, the burned gases are forced out of the engine.

Some motorcycles use smaller, two-stroke engines. The fuel mixture enters the cylinder and is compressed during the first stroke. It explodes at the start of the second stroke and the burned gases are pushed out at the end of the stroke.

Steam turbine

A modern type of steam engine is called the steam turbine. The steam turbine is used in modern steamships, because it can go faster than other steam engines. In a steam turbine, a jet of steam flows through a small fanwheel. The fanwheel turns as the steam passes through it. It turns the ship's propeller. Turbines are also used in electric power stations to turn the large electricity generators. A type of turbine is used today in jet engines, although they do not use steam.

The first steam-driven road vehicle was built by Nicolas Cugnot in 1769. It had a boiler at the front which drove the front wheel. The vehicle was not a success. It crashed on its first journey in Paris.

PROJECT 8

The twisting trick

This experiment lets you see expansion actually taking place in an amusing way. It works like a bimetallic strip. You will need aluminum foil, tape, scissors and a pencil.

STEP 1

Stick a piece of tape, about 1 foot (30 cm) long, across a piece of aluminum foil. Cut around the tape with scissors. You will end up with a strip of foil with tape on one side.

STEP 2

Attach one end of the strip to a high shelf, using tape. Bring a lamp near the hanging strip. Make sure the heat from the lamp can reach the strip. See how it twists. The reason is that the aluminum foil expands as it is heated. However, the tape does not expand as much as the foil. This difference in expansion causes the strip to twist.

STEP 3

Make another aluminum strip with tape on one side. This time, wrap it around a pencil to make a coil. Place the coil on a flat surface.

STEP 4

Bring a desk light near, so that it shines right on the coil. Make sure the heat from the lamp reaches the coil. Watch what happens. Once again, the explanation is that the aluminum expands more than the tape, which causes the strip to twist and move about.

PROJECT 9

Heat power

Heat can be used to produce steam, which can power a boat. You will need a metal cigar tube, a cork to fit the tube's end, some strong wire, pliers, nails and a hammer, two small candles or night-lights, a piece of balsa wood and a box of matches. You will need an adult to help.

STEP 1

Make an airtight seal in the tube with the cork. Make a small hole through the cork with a nail. Cut two pieces of wire of equal length and wrap them around the tube as shown. Twist the ends of the wire together with a pair of pliers. Make sure that at least 6 inches (15 cm) of wire remains at each end.

STEP 2

Cut the balsa wood into the shape of a boat. Hammer a large nail in at each end to act as a keel. Mount the candles or night-lights side by side on top of the boat. Secure them with melted wax so that you can remove them easily. Do not light them yet.

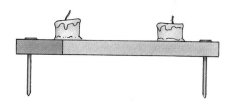

STEP 3

Wrap the wire from the cigar tube around the wood, so that the tube lies just above the candles. Fill the tube three-quarters full with hot water and cork it. Put the boat in a bathtub, or in a pond if the weather is calm. Carefully light the candles – it might be wise to ask an adult to do this. As the water heats up, steam will form in the tube. The steam builds up and is forced out through the hole in the cork. This pressure will drive the boat along.

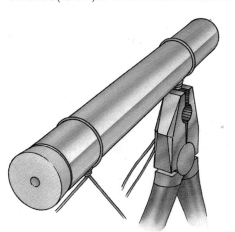

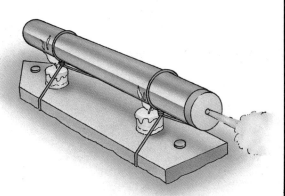

CHEMICAL CHANGES

When ice is heated, it melts and changes into water. This is called a physical change (see pages 32 and 34), and it is reversible. A completely different kind of change takes place when a piece of paper is heated. First it turns brown and becomes brittle. Then it eventually bursts into flame. It gives out a lot of heat and ends up as ash.

Energy from the past

Much of our energy comes from the fossil fuels, coal and oil. Coal is the fossilized remains of the woody parts of trees which has formed over thousands of years. Mineral oil is formed as marine plants and animals decay and are slowly compressed under layers of sediment on the sea bed.

Both coal and oil are burned in many power stations to produce steam for turbines, which in turn drive generators which produce electrical energy. This electrical energy is used to supply power to our homes. So, the energy we use to cook, heat and run our homes and industry is provided by a heat-induced chemical change.

Natural gas, which is mainly composed of methane, collects on top of oil deposits. Some of the gas used in our homes is natural gas from deposits under the sea. Ordinary coal gas is produced by burning coal in a gas-works. A smokeless fuel, coke, is produced as well as the gas. Whatever the source of the gas, it is burned in many homes both for cooking and heating.

Food energy

All plants and animals are living machines, and they, too, need fuel to supply them with energy. The fuel for living organisms is food, a source of chemical energy. Green plants can make their own food using sunlight energy to convert carbon dioxide and water into carbon compounds such as sugar. Animals have to rely on eating plants or other animals for their food.

The food we take in is digested, and the soluble products are transported around the body in the blood. In the cells of the body, the food products react chemically with oxygen to release

In coal-fired power stations, coal is burned to produce steam to run the generators. The pollution they can produce is a major cause for concern.

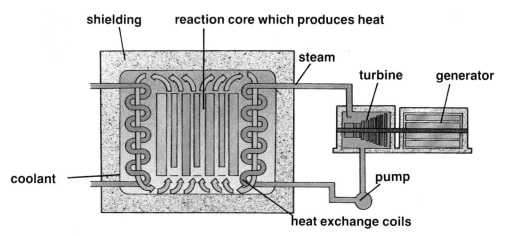

shielding   reaction core which produces heat

steam

turbine   generator

coolant

pump

heat exchange coils

Some power stations run on nuclear energy. The heat produced when large numbers of uranium atoms are split – nuclear fission – is used to produce steam and drive a turbine. This turbine is coupled to a generator to make electricity as in a coal-fired power station.

energy which is used to "run" the body. This is a form of combustion or burning. Some heat is also produced to maintain body temperature.

The unit for measuring heat and energy is the joule, but food energy is measured in *calories* (kilocalories). A woman needs about 2,000 calories a day, an adolescent about 3,000 calories and a manual worker about 3,600 calories. The more you exercise, the more energy you burn up. For example, you use about 65 calories an hour when you are sleeping, but you burn up about 300 calories an hour if you run fast. Foods such as carbohydrates (bread and cakes) and fats contain far more calories than proteins such as fish or eggs. Vegetables contain even fewer calories.

SCIENCE DISCOVERY

Units of heat

James Joule was an English scientist who was born in 1818 and died in 1889. He set out to measure exactly how much heat was produced by a certain amount of energy. Joule's apparatus was made up of a strange array of weights and pulleys. When a known weight was allowed to fall through a measured distance, it turned paddles in a container of water. Just enough energy was produced to raise the temperature of the water by a precise amount. He not only proved that heat is a form of energy, but he measured how much mechanical energy was needed to provide an exact amount of heat. The unit of energy – the joule or the B.T.U. (British Thermal Unit) – is named after him. All forms of work and energy are measured in joules. Joule was also the first person to calculate the speed of a molecule of gas, about 1,500 feet (500 m) a second for oxygen at average temperatures.

PROJECT 9

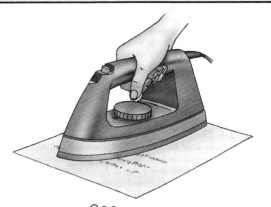

Secret writing

Heat can cause chemical changes. This means that the heat changes one substance into another. You can use this fact to make secret writing. You will need milk, paper and a wooden toothpick.

STEP 1

Dip the toothpick in the milk, and write a message on the paper. Let the paper dry. The writing will almost disappear.

STEP 2

Heat the paper by placing it in front of a bright desk light. The writing will appear. If this does not work, use an iron. Heat the iron on a wool setting, and rub it over the paper. The writing appears because the dried milk scorches more easily than the paper. This is a chemical change caused by heat.

PROJECT 10

One-way change

When a chemical change takes place, it is nearly always irreversible. You can test this for yourself quite simply. You will need an old pan, a teaspoon of sugar, a little water and a stove. Ask an adult to help.

STEP 1

Dissolve the sugar in a little water and place it on the stove. Heat the sugar until it boils. It will thicken and look like syrup and become brown in color.

STEP 1

Light the candle and allow some of the wax to drip into the bottom of the jar. Put the candle out and stand it in the melted wax. Hold it still until the wax has set and the candle is steady. Relight the candle, and put the lid on the jar. What happens to the candle?

STEP 2

Continue heating the sugar water until all the steam has disappeared. What happens to the sugar? As the sugar is heated, it burns, or caramelizes, and turns dark brown. It cannot be turned back into sugar crystals. Do not try to taste the caramel. It will be very, very hot and burn you.

STEP 2

Take the lid off the jar, relight the candle and put the lid back on the jar. What happens if you take the lid off as soon as the candle flame starts to go out?

PROJECT 11

A burning question

In order for things to burn and change, oxygen has to be present. You can prove this for yourself. You will need a candle, some matches and a jar with a lid.

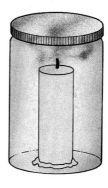

THINGS TO REMEMBER

Here are some explanations of some of the words in this book that you may find unfamiliar. In some cases, they aren't the exact scientific definitions, because many of these are very complicated. But the descriptions should help you to understand what the words mean.

ABSOLUTE ZERO The lowest possible temperature. It is just below −459°F (−273°C).

ATOM A very small particle.

BOIL To change a liquid into a gas by heating it.

CALORIE A unit used to measure the energy value of foods.

CELSIUS SCALE A temperature scale with 0° as the temperature at which water freezes and 100° as the temperature of boiling water.

CENTIGRADE SCALE Another name for the Celsius temperature scale.

CHEMICAL CHANGE A change that produces a new chemical substance.

COMBUSTION The process of burning.

CONDENSE To change a gas into a liquid by cooling it.

CONDUCTION The movement of heat through a solid body.

CONTRACT To get smaller.

CONVECTION The way heat moves through a gas or liquid as flowing currents.

ENERGY The power to do work.

EVAPORATE To change a liquid into a gas without heating it.

EXPAND To get larger.

FAHRENHEIT SCALE A temperature scale with 212° as the temperature at which water boils and 32° as the temperature at which water freezes.

FREEZE To change a liquid into a solid by cooling it.

FRICTION The force produced when two objects are rubbed together.

HEAT Energy due to vibrating atoms or molecules.

INFRARED RAYS Heat rays; the way heat travels through empty space.

INSULATOR A material through which heat and electricity cannot flow easily.

INTERNAL COMBUSTION ENGINE An engine that burns fuel to provide power.

JOULE A unit, also known as a B.T.U. or British Thermal Unit, used to measure energy and work.

KELVIN SCALE A temperature scale based on absolute zero −459°F (−273°C), 0 K.

KINETIC ENERGY The energy of movement.

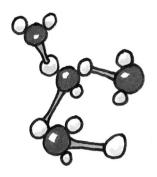

MOLECULE A tiny particle that is made up of atoms.

PHYSICAL CHANGE A change that can be reversed by heating or cooling.

RADIATION Energy that can travel through empty space as waves.

SOLIDIFY To become hard or solid when cooled.

STEAM ENGINE An engine that gets its power from hot steam.

TEMPERATURE The degree of hotness or coldness of something.

THERMOMETER An instrument for measuring temperature.

THERMOSTAT An instrument that maintains an object at a constant temperature.

VACUUM BOTTLE A container consisting of two glass walls with no air between, that keeps liquids at a steady temperature for a long time.

VIBRATE To move back and forth quickly.

MELT To change a solid into a liquid by heating it.

INDEX